In the Supermarket

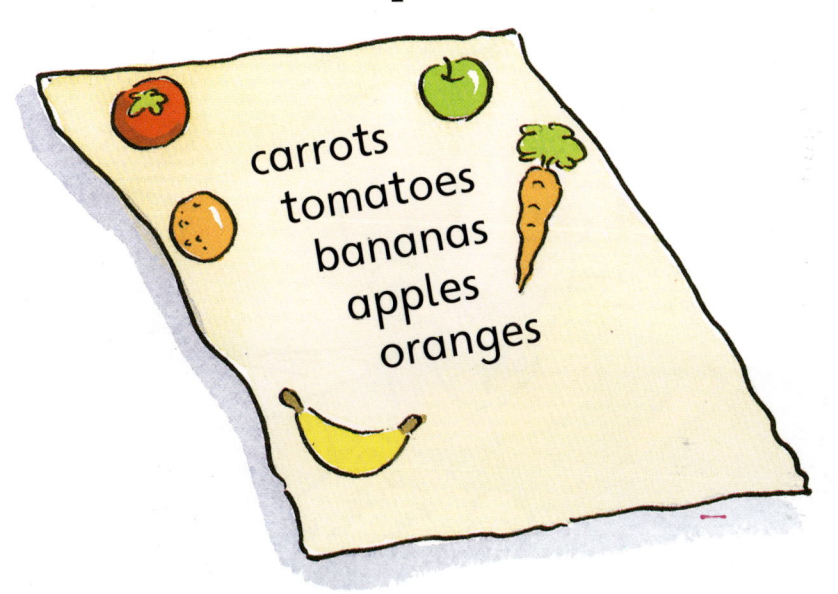

carrots
tomatoes
bananas
apples
oranges

Story by Jeanne Holloway
Illustrations by Andy Cooke

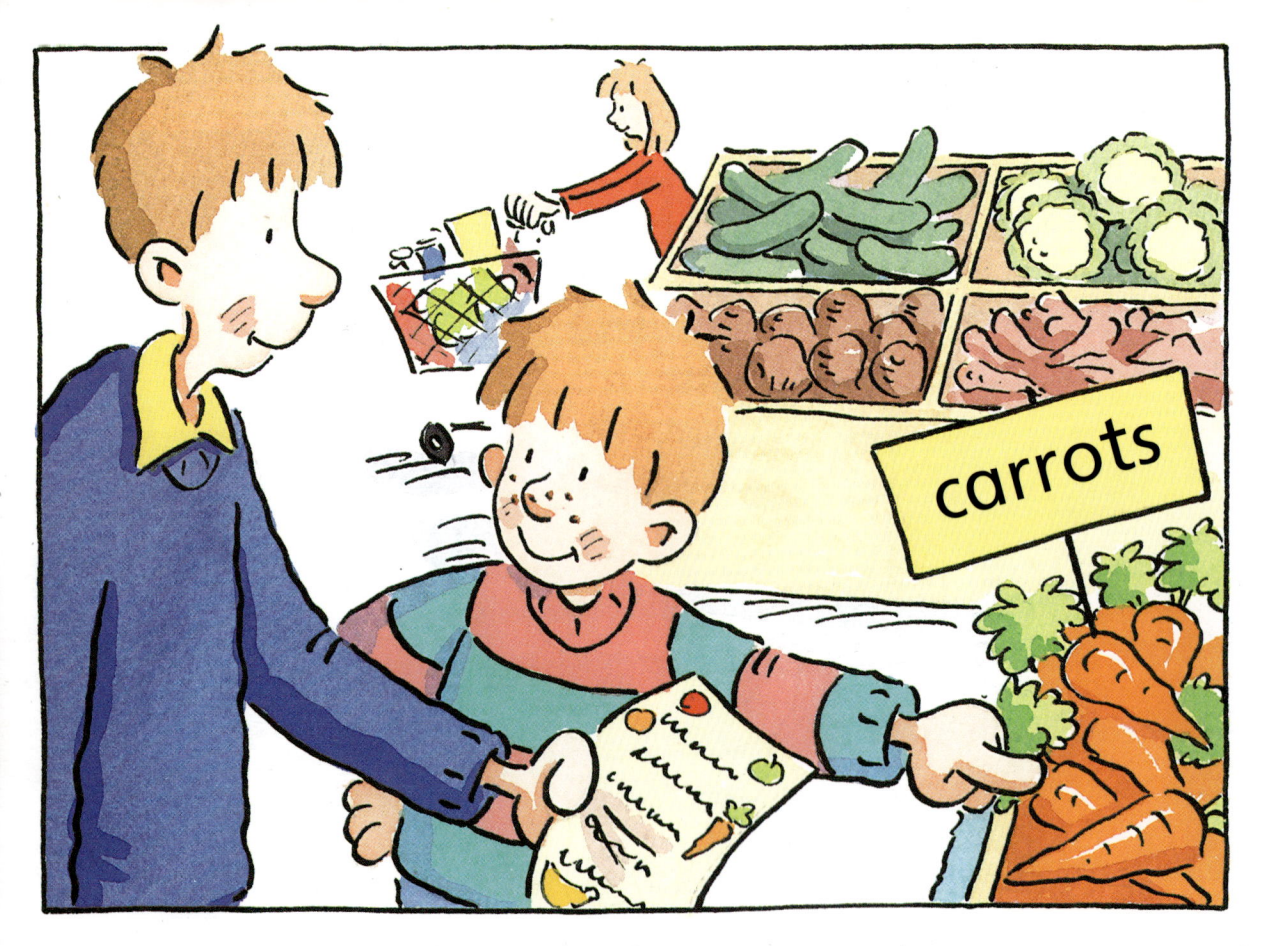

I found the carrots.

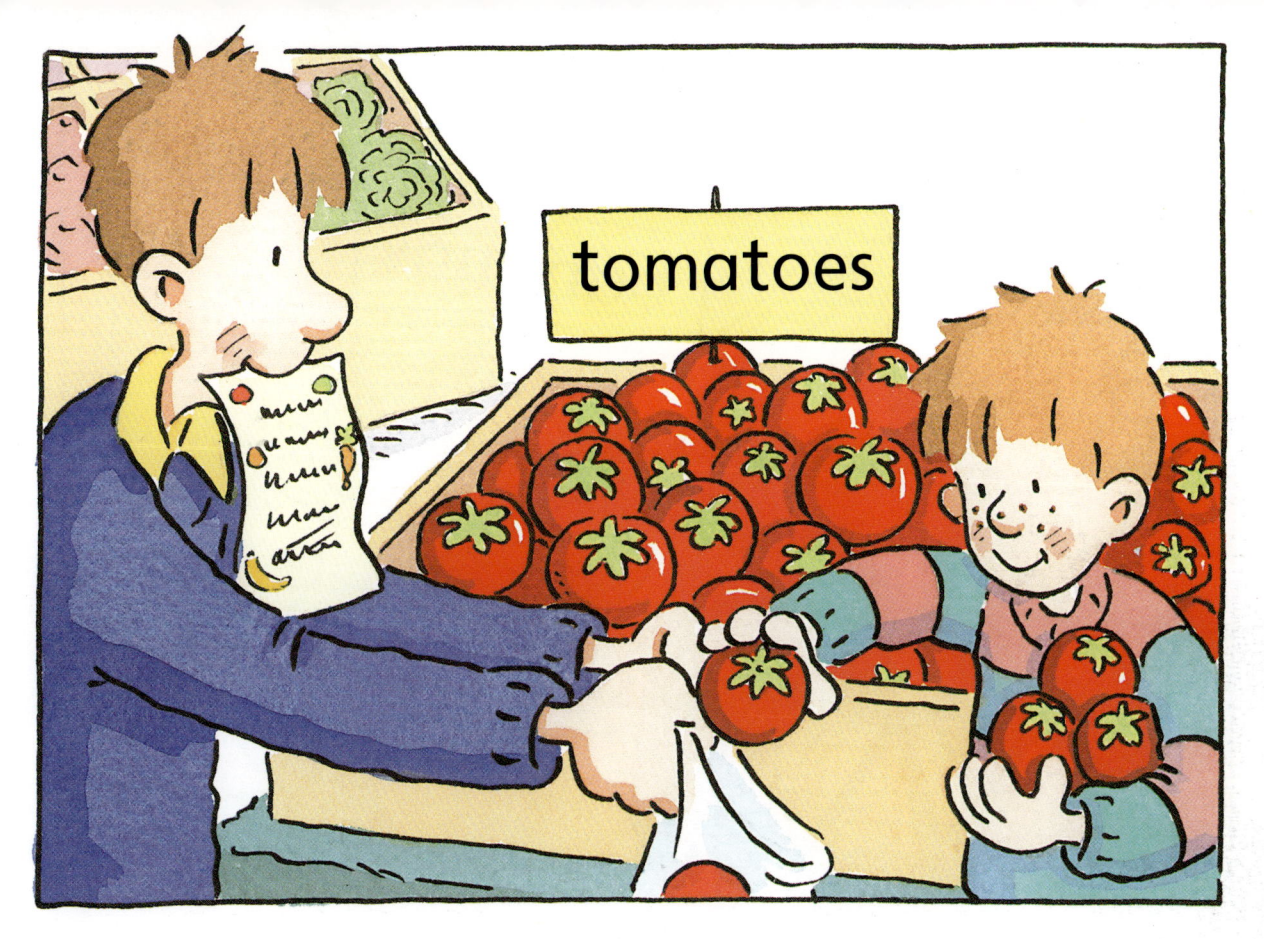

I found the tomatoes.

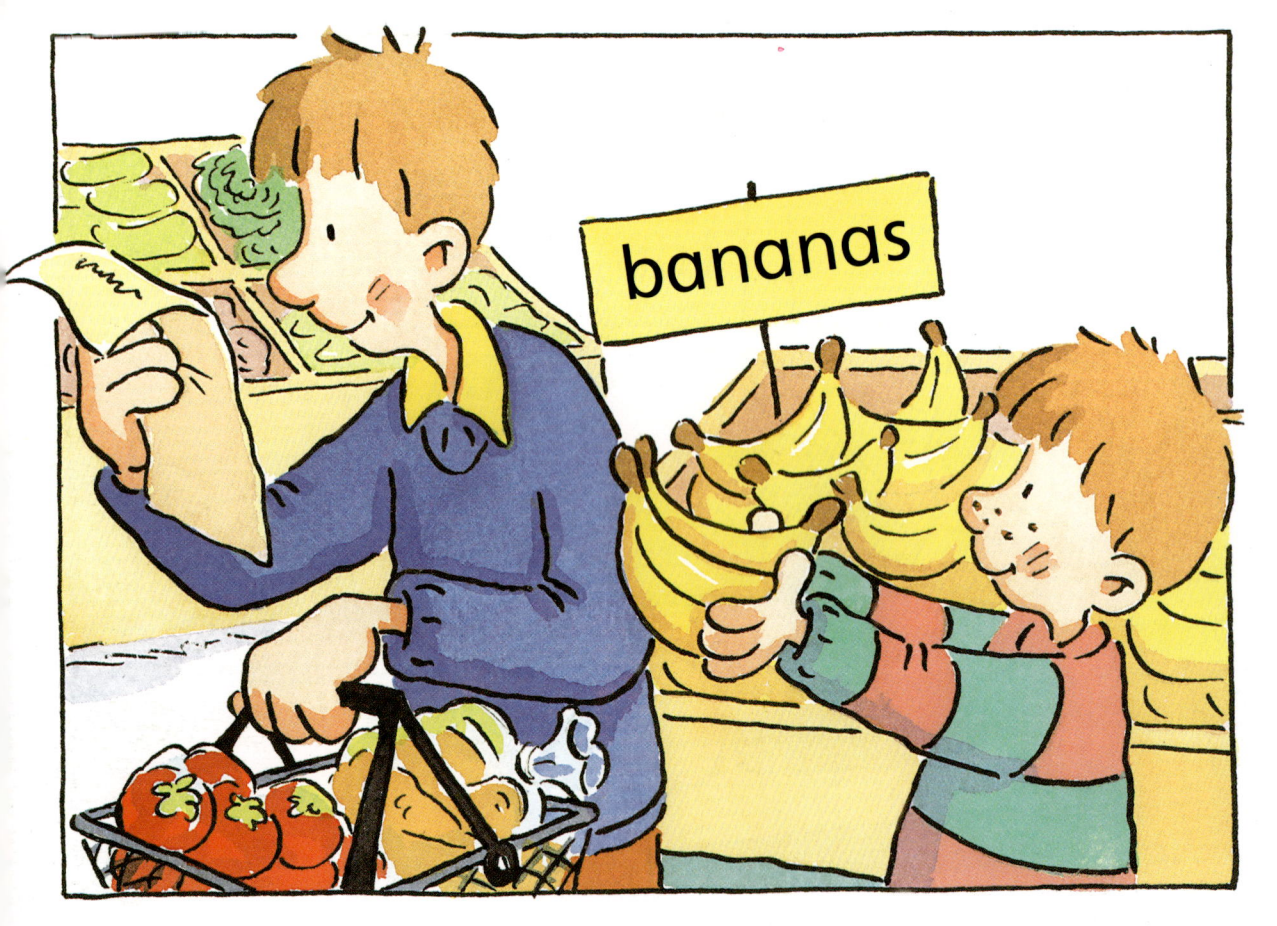

I found the bananas.

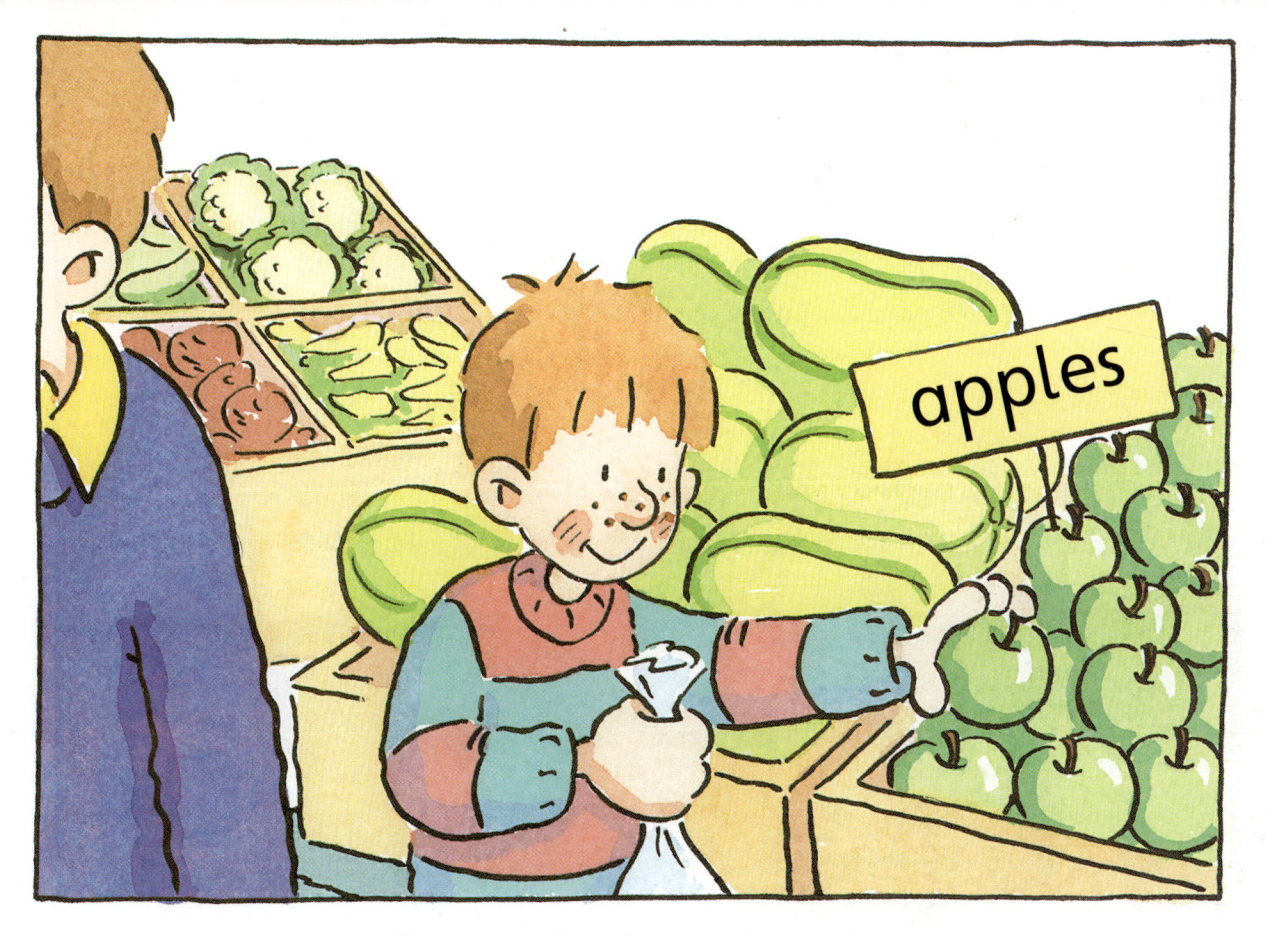

I found the apples.

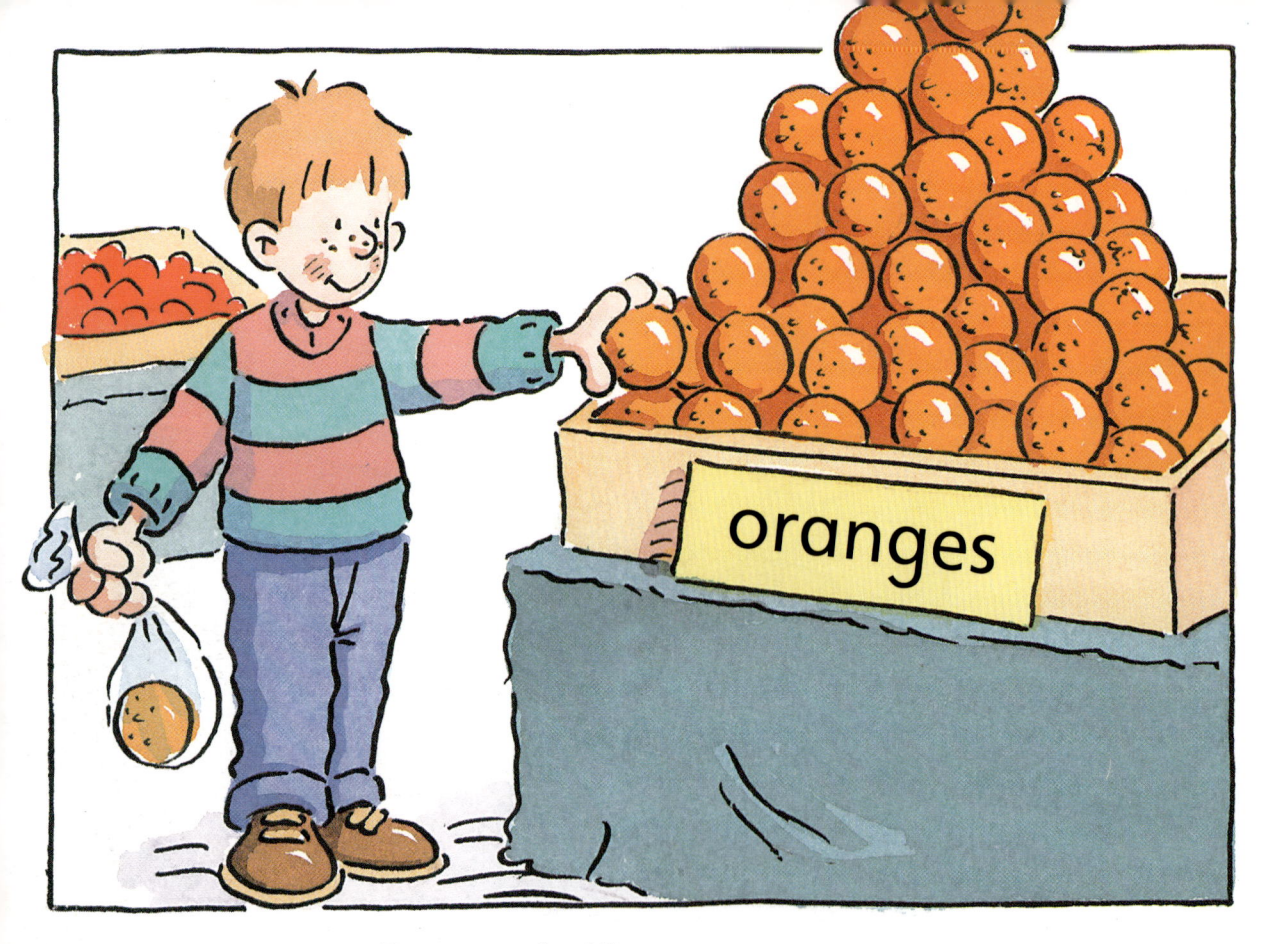

I found the oranges.

Crash!

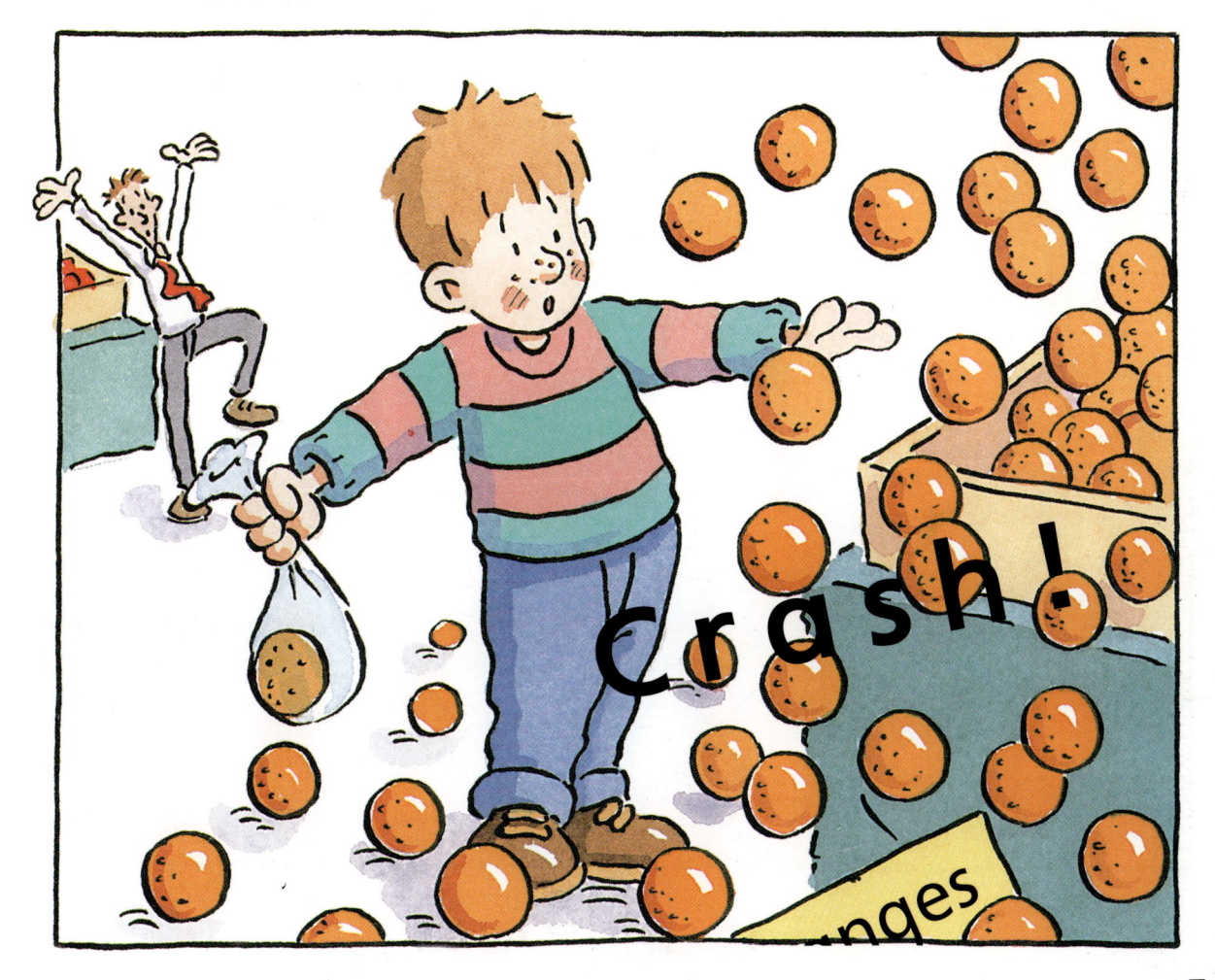

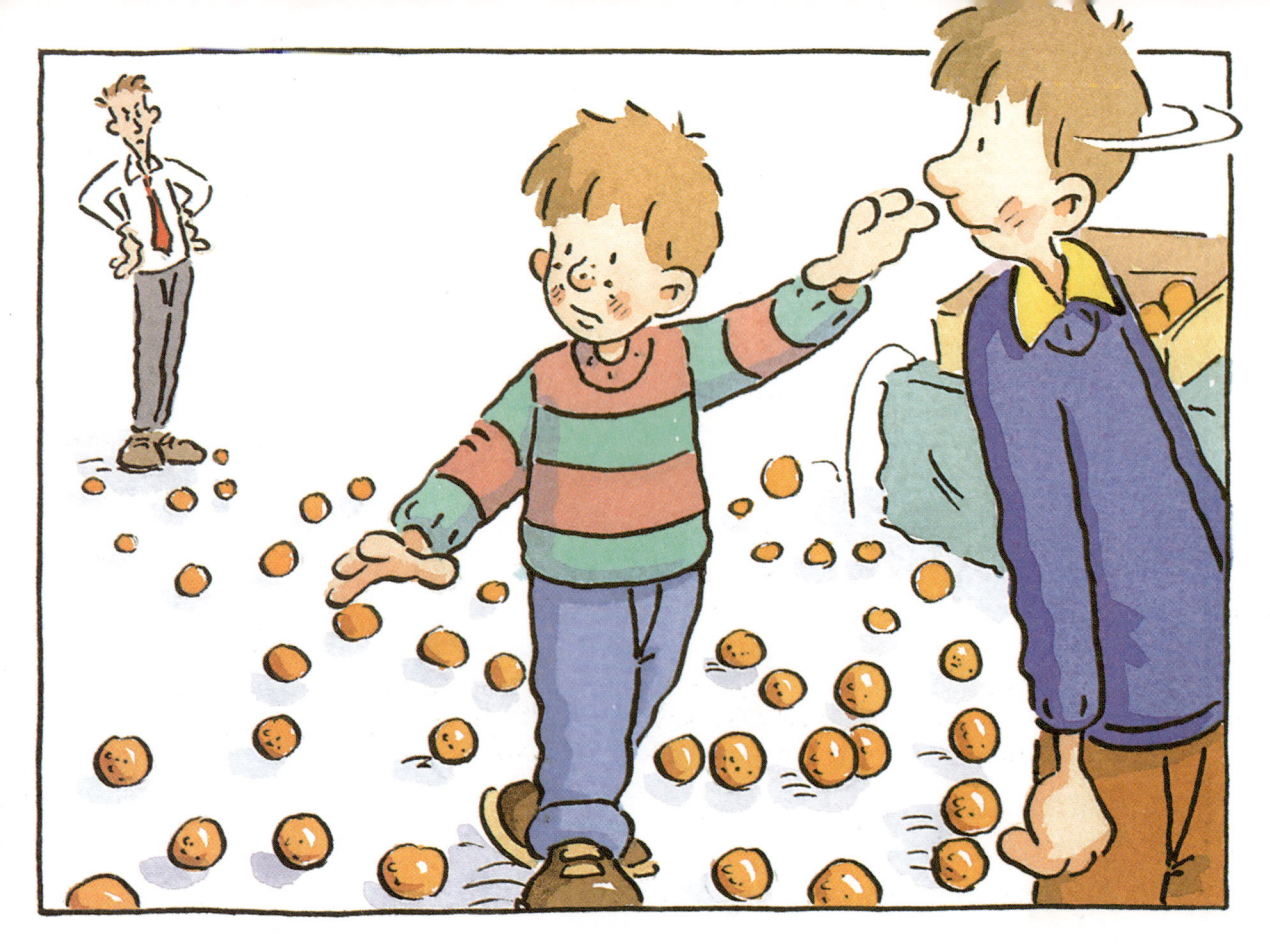

I found Dad!